H

Wheat Free

Dog Treat Recipes

Wheat Free Treats to Make for Your Dog

©Briba Publishing

"If I had a pound for every time my dog made me smile, I'd be a millionaire."

~ Steph Harris

Contents

Introduction

The terms 'wheat' and 'gluten' are often thought to mean the same thing, but they are **not** the same.

Gluten is a protein found in wheat, barley and rye. While all wheat contains gluten, not all gluten comes from wheat. So, if your dog needs a *gluten* free diet please be careful and do your research before making dog treats as other ingredients may contain gluten.

If you are reading this book you will, most probably, already know that dogs can get wheat allergies, in fact you may already ***know*** that your dog is allergic to food containing wheat.

The fact is a lot of dogs at some time in their life, have allergic reactions resulting in some sort of skin problems. As wheat is a common problem, it is one of the first things you need to investigate if you suspect your dog has an allergy of any kind.

Dogs who are suffering with skin and coat problems like itchy, red, flaky skin, and a dull coat could possibly have a food allergy.

However, it is important to visit your Vet to make sure there are no other underlying conditions that are causing his symptoms such as mite infestation, flea allergies etc.

Please don't guess – make sure!

Food allergies will account for only about 10% of a dog's allergy problems, but they are easily treatable once your dog has been diagnosed.

As you obviously care about your dog you will be sensitive to any changes to your dog's health so if you see any of the symptoms listed below it could be possible that your dog has an allergy of some kind;

- Itchy and very dry skin
- Head shaking
- Ear inflammation
- Licking front paws
- Rubbing face on carpet
- Vomiting
- Diarrhoea
- Flatulence
- Sneezing

Dogs can *develop* a food allergy; he is not necessarily born with it; just as humans can develop allergies at any time in their life.

Or you may just want to eliminate wheat from your dog's diet, it could be that you and your family don't eat wheat so you only have wheat free ingredients in your house.

For whatever reason you want to feed your dog a wheat free diet, I hope these Wheat Free Dog Treat Recipes will help to give you some ideas.

All my Dog Treat Recipe Books contain ideas that you can easily change around to include things your dog loves – you don't have to stick rigorously to the recipes.

Note: The weights in this book use American 'cups'. There is a conversion chart at the end of the book for those in UK but I simply bought a set of measurement cups from one of the pound shops (yes, you guessed it – for £1…) to make life easier.

If you are looking for a more general book of Dog Treat Recipes that you can change around to make the recipes wheat free you can find my first two books on Amazon – just type my name into the search bar.

I have left a number of pages blanks so you have room to make notes, write your own recipes – whatever you want to use them for.

This next section is included in the first book in the series but I feel it is worth repeating the information here.

No Grains

Just because your dog doesn't tolerate grains, that shouldn't stop you from making some special treats for him from 'normal' recipe books. You just need to substitute regular flour with one of the grain free alternatives available.

Below are some you could use instead

Rice flour
Quinoa
Tapioca
Oat flour (make your own by blitzing oats in a food processor)
Amaranth
Potato flour
Millet flour
Coconut flour
Gram (or Chickpea) flour

Sometimes these alternatives don't bind ingredients together as well as flours made with grain, so experiment with the ingredients. Use a beaten egg or some melted coconut oil to help to bind the ingredients together.

You may also need to experiment a little with the amount of grain free flour you use if you are substituting wheat flour with a grain free alternative. Add the substitute flour slowly (you may need less) or add more water to get the right consistency for the recipe you are making.

*"Dogs feel very strongly that they should always
go with you in the car, in case the need should arise for them
to bark violently at nothing right in your ear."*

~ Dave Barry

Coconut Oil

There are a variety of oils you can use to benefit your dog's health, each with different advantages. Coconut oil is my favorite and the one I use regularly in the dog treats I make.

Coconut oil consists of more than 90% saturated fats. Most of the saturated fats in coconut oil are Medium Chain Triglycerides (MCTs) which are good for you.

Although there is currently no definitive scientific proof, if fed regularly to your dog, it is said coconut oil *may* help:

- ❀ ...reduce allergic reactions and improves skin health

- ❀ ...encourage sleek and shiny coats

- ❀ ...prevent and treat yeast and fungal infections

- ❀ ...clear up skin conditions such as eczema, contact dermatitis and itchy skin

- ❀ ...the healing of cuts, wounds, hot spots, dry skin and hair, bites and stings when applied topically

- ❀ ...improve digestion and nutrient absorption

- ☸ …healing of digestive disorders like inflammatory bowel syndrome and colitis

- ☸ …reduce or eliminate bad breath in dogs

- ☸ …prevent infection and disease because it contains powerful antibacterial, antiviral, and anti-fungal agents.

- ☸ …regulate and balance insulin and promote normal thyroid function

- ☸ …prevent or control diabetes

There are many ways you can give coconut oil to your dog; you can add it to their food, you can feed it from a spoon (lots of dogs love it, but not my girl…) or, like me, you can incorporate coconut oil in the homemade treats.

It is well worth adding coconut oil to your dog treats.

Turmeric for Your Dog

There has been a lot written about the benefits of adding turmeric to our own diet and it is thought to be an excellent addition to the diet of dogs and horses, I am definitely a convert.

Briefly, (because this book is about dogs…) after 20+ years of burning pain in my shoulders (the left one particularly), the best the doctors could offer was painkillers and the only one that did any good was a codeine based one.

I heard about a Facebook group that talks about the health benefits of turmeric and joined.

Not being a curry fan I didn't fancy making a turmeric drink (yuk!) so I bought a capsule maker from eBay, black pepper and some turmeric powder (minimum 3% curcumin content) and made capsules. After around 8 weeks I suddenly realised that I had not taken any painkillers for a month…

The Facebook group also has a lot of success stories about the use of turmeric for various problems in dogs and horses.

Just type 'Turmeric User Group' into the search bar on Facebook.

You will find lots of information on the benefits of giving turmeric to your dog and the recipe for a super paste to add to his food.

As Paula, my whippet, doesn't appreciate the taste and would rather starve than eat her food with turmeric added, I make a batch of the 'Golden Paste', put teaspoon sized blobs (using an icing bag), on a baking tray then freeze. I then bag it up. Each day I take out 4 blobs to defrost then it's one for me and one for Paula twice a day wrapped up in half a slice of ham (for both of us...). I'm sure it has contributed to Paula no longer experiencing the intermittent lameness she'd had previously.

But it's your decision if you want to give it a go. If it doesn't help it certainly won't do any harm.

Please do remember that treats are supposed to be just that – a **TREAT**, not a meal or fed continuously throughout the day.

Alvin and Luna

Banana Almond Treats

Ingredients

½ ripe banana
½ cup almond flour
¾ cup unsalted almond butter
1 egg
1 tsp. ground cinnamon

Method

Preheat your oven to 350°F.

Line a baking sheet with parchment paper and set aside.

In a medium bowl, mash the banana with a fork until smooth. Add the remaining ingredients and mix until well blended.

Spoon dollops of batter onto the prepared baking sheet and bake for about 5 minutes; turn the pan and continue baking for 5 minutes more.

Remove from the oven and let the treats cool before serving.

Store these treats in an air-tight container in the fridge for up to two weeks.

Notes

Sweet Pumpkin Dog Treats

Ingredients

1½ cups rice flour
1 cup fresh pumpkin, peeled and diced
1 cup vegetable oil
1 cup honey
1 free range egg
½ tbsp. freshly ground ginger
1 tbsp. cinnamon

Method

Preheat your oven to 350°F. Line a baking tray with parchment paper and set aside.
Add the chopped pumpkin to the water and bring to a boil; lower heat and simmer for about 7 minutes or until tender. Drain and let cool.

Transfer the pumpkin to a food processor or blender and process to a fine puree. Refrigerate until chilled.

In a mixing bowl, mix together flour, ginger, and cinnamon until well combined.
In a separate bowl, beat together the egg, vegetable oil, and honey until well blended.

Whisk the pumpkin puree into the wet ingredients until well combined.

Slowly beat the dry ingredients into the wet ingredients until well blended.

Spoon teaspoonfuls of batter onto the baking tray, spacing 1 inch apart to form small cake patties; bake in the preheated oven for about 15 minutes or until a toothpick inserted in the centre comes out clean. Allow to cool before serving.

"The only creatures that are evolved enough to convey pure love are dogs and infants."

~ Johnny Depp

Peanut Butter Balls

Ingredients

3 cups rolled oats
1 cup peanut butter (check ingredients to make
sure NO xylitol)
½ cup natural yoghurt

Method

In a large bowl, whisk together peanut butter and
yogurt to form a paste.

Stir in the oats until well coated with the yogurt
mixture.

Scoop out spoonfuls of the mixture and roll with
hands to make balls.

Arrange the balls on a baking paper lined tray and
refrigerate them for 1 hour or until chilled.

These treats can be stored in an airtight container
in the fridge for up to two weeks or in the freezer for
several months.

Little Alfie in his best sweater

Ginger Peanut Butter Snaps

Ingredients

¼ cup water
½ cup coconut flour
2 cups almond flour
3 tbsp. ground ginger
½ – ¾ cup natural peanut butter
1 tbsp. cinnamon

Method

Preheat your oven to 350°F.

In a large bowl, mix together all the ingredients and form a ball with the mixture.

Roll the ball out on a flat surface; using a cookie cutter, cut out individual treats and arrange them onto a baking tray.

Bake in the preheated oven for about 25 minutes.

Switch off the oven and leave the baked treats inside for at least 45 minutes or until crisp.

Keep in airtight container.

No-Bake Coconut Treats

These treats are great for the children to make for the family dog. No hot ovens involved, so they can make these on their own – and it doesn't matter if they eat some...

Ingredients

2 ½ cups rolled oats
2-3 tablespoons peanut butter
1/3 cup coconut oil
1/3 cup finely shredded coconut

Method

In a food processor, combine rolled oats, peanut butter, and coconut oil; process into a fine puree.

Scoop out the mixture into bite-sized pieces and roll into small balls.

Gently toss the balls into shredded coconut until well coated and arrange them on a paper-lined baking tray.

Refrigerate for at least 30 minutes before serving.

Apple and Spinach Biscuits

Ingredients

2 tbsp. water
2 handfuls of baby spinach
2 ½ cups almond flour
1 apple, cored and seeded
½ cup natural unsalted almond butter or peanut butter
½ tsp. cinnamon

Method

Preheat your oven to 400°F.

Using your hands, mix together all the ingredients in a bowl to form dough. Roll the dough into a ball.

Lightly dust a clean surface with coconut or almond flour and roll out the dough flat.

With a dog-shaped cookie cutter, cut out the dough into biscuits and arrange them on a cookie sheet.

Bake in the preheated oven for about 25 minutes; rotate the sheet and lower temperature to 350°F.

Continue baking for 15 minutes more or until crisp. Remove the cookies from oven and cool completely before serving.

Thorns may hurt you,

Men may desert you,

Sunlight could turn to fog,

But you're never friendless, ever

If you share your life with a DOG

~ Author Unknown

Sweet Potato Dog Cookies

Ingredients

1 cup + 2 tbsp. sweet potato puree
1 ½ cup coconut flour
½ cup coconut oil
4 organic eggs
½ cup peanut butter
2 tsp. dried parsley
1/3 cup shredded carrots

Method

Preheat your oven to 350°F.

Combine all the ingredients in a mixing bowl to form dough.

Roll the dough in a ball and roll it flat on a flat work surface.

With a cookie cutter, cut out cookies; transfer them to a paper-lined baking sheet and bake in the preheated oven for about 15 minutes or until hard.

Let cool before serving.

Coconut Butter Strawberry Dog Ice Cream

Ingredients

1 cup fresh strawberries
½ cup pure coconut butter
32 oz. tub plain yogurt

Method

Add coconut butter, strawberries, and yogurt to a blender and blend until very smooth.

Pour the mixture into a freezer-safe container (an old ice cream tub washed out is perfect), cover and put in freezer for at least 6 hours or until frozen.

Serve single serving scoop of ice cream in your dog's bowl and store the rest in the freezer until needed.

Perfect for hot days.

Coconut Soft Dog Biscuits

Ingredients

6 tbsp. coconut flour
¼ cup coconut oil, melted
3 tbsp. apple sauce or 2 pureed bananas
2 eggs
½ cup mashed sweet potato
1 tsp. raw honey

Method

Preheat oven to 350°F.

In a food processor, combine eggs, mashed sweet potato, honey, melted oil, and applesauce or pureed bananas. Pulse until smooth.

Slowly pulse in coconut flour until well combined.

Spread the batter onto a paper-lined baking sheet.

Bake in the preheated oven for about 20 minutes. Remove from oven and score into small squares.

Continue baking for about 10 minutes more or until lightly browned.

Cool slightly before cutting into squares.

When I needed a hand, I found your paw…

Grain Free Dog Squares

Ingredients

2 tbsp. flaxseed meal
½ cup chicken broth (stock)
⅓ cup coconut flour
1⅓ cup tapioca flour
½ cup fat or oil of choice
2 tbsp. nutritional yeast

Method

Preheat your oven to 400°F.

Add chicken broth to a pot and bring to a gentle boil.

In a mixing bowl, mix coconut flour, tapioca flour, flax meal and yeast until well blended.

Add the boiled broth to the flour mixture and stir to combine well.

Roll out the dough on a flat surface and cut into small squares; bake for about 15 minutes.

Cool before serving.

Being a Mother doesn't mean being related by blood

It means loving unconditionally with all your heart

And if it means you love your dog, that's good

He's your friend, your protector, your family, may you never be apart

--

Protein Puppy Cakes

Ingredients

¼ cup rolled oats
1 ¾ cup garbanzo bean flour
1 large egg
3 tablespoons peanut butter
1 medium banana, mashed

Method

Preheat your oven to 300°F.

Beat together egg, peanut butter, and banana in a small bowl until well blended.

Combine rolled oats and flour in a medium bowl; stir in the wet ingredients until the dough comes together.

Roll out the dough to about ¼ inch thickness then, with a cookie cutter, cut the cookies and arrange them on a baking paper lined baking sheet.

Bake in the preheated oven for about 40 minutes or until browned.

Let the cookies cool completely before serving.

Cheesy Dog Chunks

Ingredients

7-9 tbsp. of water
½ cup of olive oil
1¼ cups shredded (grated) cheddar cheese
2 cups of rice flour

Method

Preheat your oven to 325°F.

In a bowl, mix together all the ingredients to form dough.

Roll out the dough onto lightly floured water.

Cut the dough into cookies of desired shapes and place on a paper-lined baking sheet and bake for about 15 minutes or until browned.

Turn off the oven and let the cookies cool completely before removing so they will harden slightly. Store in an airtight container or freeze for later use.

Crunchy Biscuits

Ingredients

1 tbsp. beef bouillon granules
1/3 cup butter
1¾ cups cornmeal
2 cups rice flour
1 egg, beaten
¾ cup powdered milk
½ cup hot water

Method

Preheat your oven to 325°F.

In a bowl, mix together hot water, beef granules, butter and cornmeal; let the mixture stand for about 5 minutes and then stir in powdered milk.

Beat in the egg and a cup of flour until well combined.

Whisk in the remaining flour and knead to firm dough.

Lightly dust a surface with rice flour and roll out the dough. With a cookie cutter, cut out small cookies and arrange them on a baking tray lined with baking paper; bake for about 5 minutes.

Remove from oven and cool completely before serving.

Nutty Bacon Dog Treats

Ingredients

3 slices of bacon, diced
1 egg
½ cup peanut butter
3 tablespoons water
½ cup soy flour
½ cup almond flour
½ cup coconut flour

Method

Preheat oven to 300°F and line two baking sheets with parchment paper.

Fry the diced bacon until crispy. With a slotted spoon, remove the crispy bacon but save the fat. Allow the fat to cool slightly.

Add the egg, peanut butter and water to the bacon fat and mix thoroughly.

Add in the flours and mix until well combined. Stir in the crispy bacon pieces.

Roll out the dough on a lightly floured surface to about ¼" thick. Using a cookie cutter, cut out your shapes and arrange on baking sheets.

Bake in the oven for 12-15 minutes or until lightly browned.

Allow to cool then store in an airtight container.

The very glamorous Dora

If I Didn't Have a Dog…

If I didn't have a dog I could walk round my garden barefoot without a worry

My house would have some carpets instead of tiles

My clothes and furniture would be hair free

I could go on long holidays

No unexpected vet bills

I could stay out all night with no worries

The most used words in my vocabulary would not be leave, sit, stay, get down and come here

I could have my favourite chair back

No more disturbed nights

No more walking in freezing cold weather

My house would look tidy for more than 10 minutes

But, if I didn't have a dog...

How very empty and lonely my life would be

~ Author Unknown

Carob Cookies

Ingredients

1 cup white rice flour
½ cup carob powder
1 teaspoon cinnamon
1 teaspoon vanilla extract
½ cup coconut oil, melted
Water as needed

Method

Preheat oven to 350° F and line a baking sheet with parchment paper or a silicone baking mat.

Mix all dry ingredients in a large bowl and add melted coconut oil. Next add water gradually until you get a good consistency. Knead until dough is smooth.

Roll on a heavily floured surface (I use half carob powder, half rice flour) to around ¼ inch thick and cut with small cookie cutter of your choice. Place on prepared baking sheet.

Bake for 10 to 15 minutes.

Turn off the oven and allow to cool before removing.

Notes

*"If you want the best seat in the house,
you'll have to move the dog."*

Meaty Treats

Ingredients

½ cup chicken or beef broth
½ cup fat or oil of choice (bacon fat, coconut oil, olive oil, etc.)
1½ cup tapioca flour
½ cup coconut flour
2 tablespoons brewers or nutritional yeast
2 tablespoons flax meal (sometimes called ground flax or milled linseed)
1 tbsp. fresh parsley (optional but good for bad breath)

Method

Preheat oven to 350°F.

In a small pot over medium heat, bring the chicken broth and fat/oil to a boil.

While that is coming to a boil, mix tapioca flour, coconut flour, brewers yeast, flax meal and parsley (if using) in a medium bowl.

Once the broth/fat mixture comes to a boil, remove from heat and add to the flour bowl and mix well.

Using a teaspoon, make small balls then flatten a little and place on a parchment lined baking sheet.

Bake for 25 minutes. When the 25 minutes are up, turn the oven off, open the door a little and leave in the oven until cool (about 10-15 more minutes).

Canine Crunch

Ingredients

1 tbsp. beef bouillon granules
2 tbsp. butter or coconut oil
1¾ cups cornmeal (polenta)
2 cups rice flour
1 egg, beaten
¾ cup powdered milk
½ cup hot water

Method

Preheat your oven to 325°F.

In a bowl, mix together hot water, beef granules, butter (or coconut oil) and cornmeal; let the mixture stand for about 5 minutes and then stir in powdered milk.

Beat in the egg and a cup of flour until well combined.

Stir in as much of the remaining flour as you need to achieve a firm dough. Knead until combined.

Lightly dust a surface with rice flour and roll out the dough. With a cookie cutter, cut out small cookies and arrange them on a baking tray lined with baking paper; bake for about 5 minutes.

Remove from oven and cool completely before serving.

"I feel sorry for those who don't have a dog,

I hear they have to pick up any food they drop on the floor..."

Dog Truffles

Ingredients

4 oz. liver
1 cup shredded cheddar cheese
1 large potato
1 lb. ground (minced) beef
1 egg

Method

Spread the liver out on a greased baking tray.
Place in oven at 200°F until dried out.

Meanwhile, bring a pan of water to a gentle boil;
peel and chop the potao and add to the water.
Cook until tender; drain and stir in cheese.

Mash until cheese is melted into the potato.

Brown ground beef in a pan over medium heat;
drain off fat and add the beef to the potato mixture.
Stir until well combined.

Refrigerate until chilled.

When the liver is completely died out, place into a
food processor or blender and process until
powdered. Transfer the powder to a shallow dish.

Turn the oven up to 300°F.

In a large bowl mix the egg into the beef and potato
mixture then roll to form small balls. Roll the balls

into the liver powder and arrange them on a baking sheet; bake for about 20 minutes.

Remove from oven and let cool completely before serving.

Rosemary Lemon Chicken Treats

Ingredients

1 cooked chicken breast, finely chopped
1¼ cup oat flour
1/3 cup milk
1 tsp. lemon juice
½ tsp. crushed dried rosemary

Method

Preheat your oven to 300°F.

Line a baking sheet with baking paper.

Mix together all the ingredients in a large bowl; knead the dough until it comes together. Roll out on a surface lightly dusted with oat flour.

Using your chosen cookie cutter, cut the dough into small cookies and arrange on the baking sheet; bake for about 25 minutes.

Remove from oven and let cool completely before serving.

Store extra in the refrigerator or freeze until required.

Anyone who has never tasted soap, has never washed a dog

~ Franklin P Jones

Bacon Dog Treats

Ingredients

3 tablespoons water
3 slices of thinly sliced bacon
1/3 cup peanut butter
1 egg
1 cup whole almond flour
½ cup coconut flour
1 tablespoon maple syrup

Method

Preheat your oven to 300°F. Line two baking sheets with baking paper and set aside.

In a frying pan, fry bacon until crispy; transfer the cooked bacon to a plate, reserving fat in the pan.

Add the egg, maple syrup, peanut butter, and water to the pan, stir well. Mix in flours until well blended; stir in bacon and roll the dough out on a lightly floured working surface.

Cut the dough into desired shapes and bake for about 15 minutes or until browned on the outside.

Cool before serving.

Dog Carob Crunchers

Ingredients

1 cup white rice flour
¾ cup water
1 teaspoon vanilla extract
1 teaspoon cinnamon
½ cup carob powder

Method

Preheat your oven to 350°F. Line a baking sheet with baking paper and set aside.

In a bowl, mix together all the ingredients to form dough.

Roll the dough onto a lightly floured surface and cut with a cookie cutter into small cookies.

Arrange them on the prepared baking sheet and bake for about 15 minutes or until the cookies begin to crackle.

Turn off the oven and leave inside until oven is cold.

Store in airtight container or freeze until required.

"Dogs lives are too short. Their only fault, really..."

Apple and Cheese Dog Biscuits

Ingredients

2 tablespoons olive oil
1/3 cup unsweetened applesauce
¼ cup grated Parmesan cheese
1/3 cup shredded cheddar
½ cup old-fashioned oatmeal
2 cups coconut flour
Water as needed

Method

Preheat your oven to 350°F.

Line a baking sheet with baking paper and set aside.

Mix together all the ingredients in a mixing bowl with about 3 tablespoons of water.

Roll out the dough on a floured surface to ¼-inch thickness and, using your chosen cookie cutter, cut into shaped cookies.

Arrange the cookies about 1 inch apart on the baking sheet and bake for about 30 minutes or until firm and browned. Cool the biscuits completely before serving.

Blueberry Dog Bites

Ingredients

1½ cups oat flour
¾ cup flax meal (ground linseed in UK)
2 ½ cups quinoa flour
1 large egg
¼ cup olive oil
½ cup frozen blueberries
Water as needed

Method

Preheat your oven to 350°F. Line a baking sheet with parchment paper and set aside.

Mix together all the ingredients in a mixing bowl with about 3 tablespoons of water, you may need more or less so add water gradually.

Roll out the dough on a floured surface to ¼-inch thickness and cut into shaped cookies.

Arrange the cookies about 1 inch apart on the baking sheet and bake for about 30 minutes or until firm and browned.

Cool the biscuits completely before serving. Store the biscuits in an airtight container for up to two weeks or freeze until required.

If you can look at a puppy and not feel love - you must be a cat...

~ Author Unknown

Carrot and Chia Dog Treats

Ingredients

¼ cup chia seeds
½ cup flax meal (ground linseed)
1 cup rice flour
1 cup almond flour
2 tablespoons maple syrup
2 melted tablespoons coconut oil
2/3 cup water
1/3 cup butter
2 carrots, grated

Method

Preheat your oven to 350°F. Line a baking sheet with baking paper and set aside.

In a medium bowl, combine chia seeds, flax meal and flours.

In a separate bowl, whisk together syrup, oil, water, and butter; stir in the carrots and pour into the dry ingredients. Stir until dough comes together.

Roll the dough out on a lightly floured surface to ¼-inch thickness and cut out cookies of your desired shapes.

Arrange the biscuits on a baking sheet and bake in the preheated oven for about 40 minutes.

Cool the biscuits completely before serving. Store the biscuits in an air-tight container up to two weeks or in the freezer until required.

Cheesy Meat Bites

Ingredients

2 tablespoons melted coconut oil
1 large egg
¾ cup beef broth
½ cup dried milk
¾ cup cornmeal or polenta
1½ cups almond flour
¼ cup nutritional yeast
2/3 cup shredded cheddar cheese

Method

Preheat the oven to 350°F.

Line 2 shallow baking sheets with parchment paper.

In a medium bowl, combine cornmeal, flour, dry milk, and yeast until well combined. Stir in cheddar cheese.

In a small bowl, whisk together the egg, broth and oil; stir the wet ingredients into the dry ingredients until a dough comes together. You may need to add a little more water or flour to achieve the right consistency.

On a lightly floured surface, roll out the dough to ¼-inch thickness and cut into small biscuits.

Arrange the biscuits on a baking sheet and bake for about 35 minutes or until browned.

Cool the biscuits before serving. Freeze until required.

Chicken Jerky

A healthy alternative to store bought chews.

Ingredients

Chicken breasts – as many as you like

Method

Preheat your oven to 200°F.

Slice the chicken breasts into very thin strips.

Arrange the chicken strips on a baking sheet and bake in the preheated oven for about 2 hours or until hard and dry.

Remove the chicken from oven and let cool before serving.

Definitely NO bath for me...

Veggie and Fruit Dog Squares

Ingredients

1 cup carrots, shredded (minced)
1 medium banana
1 small sweet potato
1 cup of rolled oats
2 cups of almond flour
1/3 cup of water
½ cup unsweetened applesauce

Method

Preheat your oven to 350°F.

Microwave the sweet potato for about 10 minutes or until soft; let cool in a bowl.

In a mixing bowl, mash together the cooked potato and banana until smooth; stir in oats, flour, carrots, water and applesauce. Knead to a soft dough.

Onto a lightly floured surface, roll out the dough to a 1/8-inch thickness and cut into small squares.

Bake in the preheated oven for about 25 minutes.

Let cool before serving; store the leftovers in the fridge for up to two weeks or in the freeze until required.

Peanut Fresh Breath Biscuits

Ingredients

1 cup rolled oats
2 cups rice flour
1 tbsp. dried parsley (or 2 tbsp. fresh chopped parsley)
2 eggs
½ cup dried milk
1 cup peanut butter
Water as needed

Method

Preheat oven to 300°F. Line a baking sheet with parchment paper or grease it well.

Mix together all the dry ingredients in a large bowl. In a small bowl, beat the eggs lightly then add the peanut butter. Pour the wet ingredients over the dry and mix well. Add as much water as needed to achieve the desired consistency. It should be stiff enough to roll out.

Knead for a few minutes until you have a smooth ball of dough or you could even use a mixer for faster results. Roll out on a lightly floured board to around ½ thick. Using a cookie cutter cut into shapes.

Bake for 30 minutes or until golden. If you want softer dog treats, take them out 10 minutes earlier.

Allow to cool before putting into an airtight container or freeze for later.

Note: For even better biscuits, use fresh parsley finely chopped instead of dried.

Every once in a while a dog comes into your life and changes everything…

Baked Chicken Biscuits

Ingredients

1 lb chicken giblets
4 tbsp coconut oil
2 eggs
2 cups coconut flour
1 cup cornmeal

Method

Preheat oven to 450°F. Line a baking sheet with parchment paper or grease it well.

Place the chicken giblets in a large saucepan then cover with water and bring to the boil. Turn the heat down and simmer for around 15 minutes with the lid on the pan.

Remove giblets from pan and allow to cool slightly.

Add the cooked giblets, coconut oil, and eggs. Blend until the ingredients are mixed but still with some texture.

Pour mixture into a large mixing bowl, add the flour and cornmeal, and mix thoroughly.

Drop teaspoonfuls of the mixture onto the greased baking sheet leaving room between for the biscuits to expand a little. Bake for 20 minutes.

Store the biscuits in the freezer and take out as needed. They can be stored for up to a week in an airtight container in the refrigerator.

Chicken Liver and Oat Training Treats

These treats are ideal for using as rewards at training classes as the liver gives off a tempting (to your dog…) smell. Most dogs will do anything for these.

Ingredients

1 pack chicken livers
1 tsp dried parsley
Porridge oats as required

Method

Preheat oven to 350°F.

Blitz the chicken livers and parsley until quite runny – a hand blender will do the job perfectly.

Add porridge oats to liver and parsley mixture until really stiff.

Line a cake tin with parchment paper or grease really well.

Spoon the mixture in, pressing down well to make an even layer.

Bake in pre-heated oven for around 25-30 minutes.

Cut into very small squares before it cools completely.

Once completely cool, place in separate potions in freezer bags. Freeze immediately because these treats don't last long in the refrigerator.

Remove from freezer and put into refrigerator the day before required.

Cheese and Oaty Balls

Ingredients

2 cups oat flour (you can make your own by blitzing pots in a blender)
1 cup shredded Cheddar cheese
4 tbsps. coconut oil
2 eggs
½ cup oats

Method

Preheat oven to 350°F and line a baking sheet with parchment paper or grease well.

Mix all ingredients in a large bowl until well combined.

With damp hands so dough won't stick too much, roll into 1 inch balls. Place balls onto the prepared baking sheet.

Press each ball down lightly with the back of a fork.

Bake for 10 minutes. When you see the cheese bubble, remove from oven. Cool and refrigerate.

These can be frozen for later use.

"Without my dog my wallet would be full my house would be clean but my heart would be empty."

~ Author Unknown

Apple and Oat Biscuits

Ingredients

½ cup plain Greek yogurt
¼ cup ground flax seed
Water as needed
1 tbsp. melted coconut oil
2½ cups oatmeal
1 apple

Method

Preheat oven to 350ºF.

Put oatmeal in a blender or food processor process until it has a flour like consistency.

Peel and core the apple removing all the seeds. Chop very finely.

Combine flour, oatmeal, and ground flax seed in a large bowl.

Fold copped apples, coconut oil and yogurt into dry ingredients, add a bit of water if   necessary to hold dough together.

Turn out onto a lightly floured board and roll to ¼ inch thick.

Cut shapes with a small cookie cutter and place on a greased cookie sheet.

Bake for 15-20 minutes.

Cool before storing in an airtight container. You can freeze these if you make a large batch.

Coconut and Cinnamon Pupcakes

Ingredients

1 cup coconut flour
½ cup shredded coconut (you could use desiccated coconut)
4 eggs
1 tsp cinnamon
2 tbsps. almond milk
1 tbsps. milled flax seed

Method

Preheat oven to 350°F.

Mix eggs and almond milk together.

Put all remaining ingredients in a large bowl and stir well to combine. Add the wet ingredients to the bowl and mix again, you could use a food processor to make it easier.

Spoon mixture into paper cupcake cases and bake for around 20-25 minutes.

Allow to cool before storing in an airtight container. These will freeze well too.

Liver Lovelies

Ingredients

1¼ lbs liver
1½ cups oats
3 tbsps. potato flour
1 cup cooked barley
2 eggs
3 tablespoons peanut butter
1 clove garlic
1 tbsp. coconut oil

Method

Pre-heat oven to 350°F.

Blend liver and garlic clove until it is a smooth paste. Add the eggs and peanut butter and blend again until smooth.

In separate bowl mix together the oats, potato flour, and cooked barley. Add the blended liver mixture and coconut oil and mix until ingredients are well combined.

Pour the mixture into a greased 9 x 9 baking dish and bake for around 20 minutes or until cooked.

Cool then cut into treat sized pieces and store in the freezer until needed.

Note: This recipe makes a lot of treats so you could halve the ingredients if you want to make a smaller batch.

"Nothing in the world is friendlier than a wet dog."

~ Ambrose Bierce

Sardine Snacks

Ingredients

2 cups cornmeal (polenta)
½ cup oat flour
2 tsp baking powder
1 tin sardines in oil
1 cup water

Method

Preheat oven to 350°F

Put all dry ingredients in a bowl and stir to combine.

Put sardines in oil into a bowl and mash with a fork. At this stage you can choose if you want to leave the sardines in chunks or beat until quite smooth.

Add the sardines to the dry ingredients and mix well, adding enough water to form a dough.

Using a teaspoon, shape the dough into small balls and place on a well-greased baking tray about ½ inch apart.

Bake in the oven for around 35-30 minutes or until nicely golden. Remove and cool before storing in an airtight container or freeze.

Note: *I feel it my duty to tell you that, although my dogs have always loved these, the smell in the kitchen when they are baking is quite strong… 😊 😊*

Beef Stock Biscuits

Ingredients

2 cups oat flour
1 cup oat bran
1 tsp organic coconut oil
1 tsp cod liver oil
2 ½ cups beef broth (stock) *You could use gravy granules but check ingredient list first*

Method

Preheat oven to 350°F.

Grease baking trays with coconut oil.

Mix dry ingredients.

Melt the coconut oil then mox with cod liver oil and beef broth.

Slowly add wet ingredients to dry, while mixing, until a solid dough is formed. (Add extra water or flour if needed)

Knead on floured surface until mixture feels the right consistency to roll out.

Cut shapes and place on baking trays.

Bake for around 45 minutes. Turn the off oven and leave until oven is cold for a crunchy biscuit

"Puppies are nature's remedy for feeling unloved, plus numerous other ailments of life"

~ Richard Allan

Notes

Thank You

Thank you for buying this book.

A donation will be made to a Dog Rescue Charity from any profits from the sale of the book to help rehabilitate and rehome unloved and unwanted dog.

"Every Dog deserves a home but not every home deserves a dog…"

I hope you will enjoy making some of these treats for your dogs. Get the children involved too, they will love making treats for their best friend (and it doesn't matter if they try them too…).

Don't forget, you can use any dog treat recipe and adapt to 'Wheat Free', just swap the wheat flour to grain free. You may have to use a bit of trial and error to get the right consistency.

To see my other 'Dog Treat Recipe' books just type my name (Karen J Connell) into the Amazon search bar and a list will come up.

Finally, can I say thank you to Lisa Hobbs for allowing me to use her photographs of Alfie the whippet and Dora the Chinese Crested on the back cover and to Clare Driver for the photographs of Alvin and Luna..

Remember, Adopt don't Shop!

Your Recipes

Your Recipes

Measurement Conversions

The United States uses a different measurement system than the rest of the world. There are different units and systems of measurement for different parts of the world, so I've included a few conversions that may help you.

U.S. to metric conversions:

Quantity

1 ounce (fluid) = 29.574 milliliter
1 cup = 236.58 milliliters, or .236 liters, 140 grams (dry)
1 pint = .47 liters
1 quart = .946 liters
1 gallon = 3.785 liters

Weight

1 ounce = 28.35 grams
1 pound = 453.59 grams, or .453 kilograms

Temperature

32°Fahrenheit = 0°Celsius

250°F = Gas mark 1 & 130°C
300°F = Gas mark 2 & 150°C
325°F = Gas mark 3 & 170°C
350°F = Gas mark 4 & 180°C

375°F = Gas mark 5 & 190°C
400°F = Gas mark 6 & 200°C
425°F = Gas mark 7 & 220°C
450°F = Gas mark 8 & 230°C
475°F = Gas mark 9 & 240°C
N.B. If you have a fan oven, the temperature should be reduced by 20°C

Here are some other useful measurement conversions:

1 Cup is equal to:

½ pint
8 ounces
16 Tablespoon
48 Teaspoons
237 milliliters

1 Tablespoon is equal to:

1/16 cup
½ ounce
3 Teaspoons
15 milliliters

1 pint is equal to 2 cups, or .47 liters
1 quart is equal to 4 cups, or .946 liters
1 gallon is equal to 4 quarts, or 16 cups, or 3.79 liters

Convenient Conversions:

¼ cup is equal to 4 Tablespoons, or 2 ounces, or 59 milliliters

½ cup is equal to 8 Tablespoons, or 4 ounces, or 118 milliliters

DISCLAIMER

All information in the book is for general information purposes only.

The author has used her best efforts in preparing this information and makes no representations or warranties with respect to the accuracy, applicability or completeness of the material contained within.

The author shall in no event be held liable for losses or damages whatsoever. The author assumes no responsibility or liability for any consequences resulting directly or indirectly from any action or lack of action that you take based on the information in this document. Use of the publication and recipes therein is at your own risk.

Reproduction or translation of any part of this publication by any means, electronic or mechanical, without the permission of the author, is both forbidden and illegal. You are not permitted to share, sell, and trade or give away this document, it is for your own personal use only, unless stated otherwise.

The reader assumes full risk and responsibility for all actions taken as a result of the information contained within this book and the author will not be held responsible for any loss or damage, whether consequential, incidental, or otherwise that may result from the information presented in this book.

The author has relied on her own experiences when compiling this book and each recipe is tried and tested in her own kitchen.

By using any of the recipes in this publication, you agree that you have read the disclaimer and agree with all the terms.

.